Books by the author

Essential Skills for a Brilliant Family Dog

Book 1 Calm Down! *Step-by-Step to a Calm, Relaxed, and Brilliant Family Dog*

Book 2 Leave It! *How to teach Amazing Impulse Control to your Brilliant Family Dog*

Book 3 Let's Go! *Enjoy Companionable Walks with your Brilliant Family Dog*

Book 4 Here Boy! *Step-by-step to a Stunning Recall from your Brilliant Family Dog*

Essential Skills for your *Growly* but Brilliant Family Dog

Book 1 Why is my Dog so Growly? *Teach your fearful, aggressive, or reactive dog confidence through understanding*

Book 2 Change for your Growly Dog! *Action steps to build confidence in your fearful, aggressive, or reactive dog*

Book 3 Calm walks with your Growly Dog *Strategies and techniques for your fearful, aggressive, or reactive dog*

www.brilliantfamilydog.com/books

Essential Skills for a Brilliant Family Dog

Book 1

Calm Down!

Step-by-Step to a Calm, Relaxed, and Brilliant Family Dog

Beverley Courtney

Your free book is waiting for you!

Get the next piece of the puzzle

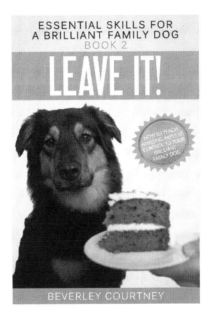

Get the second book in this series absolutely free at

www.brilliantfamilydog.com/freebook

Disclaimer

I have made every effort to make my teachings crystal clear, but we're dealing with live animals here (That's you, and your dog.) and I can't see whether you're doing it exactly right. I am unable to guarantee success, as it depends entirely on the person utilising the training programs, strategies, tools, and resources.

What I do know is that this system works!

Nothing in these books should upset or worry your dog in any way, but if your dog has a pre-existing problem of fear or aggression you should consult a force-free trainer to help. www.brilliantfamilydog.com/growly will get you started.

By the way, to simplify matters I refer to our trainee dog throughout this series as "she." "He" and "she" will both learn the exact same way. The cumbersome alternatives of "he/she" or "they" depersonalise our learner: I want her to be very real to you!

All the photos in this book are of "real" dogs – either my own, or those of students and readers (with their permission). So the reproduction quality is sometimes not the best. I have chosen the images carefully to illustrate the concepts – so we'll have to put up with some fuzziness.

Contents

Introduction
Time for a change

Coco (15 weeks) says, "If this thing is on the ground, I must need to sit on it."

You, your dog and your family have had a great outing, seeing the sights of the seaside town - the beach, the castle, the ramparts, the quaint streets, and the shops. You all are now exhausted and need to stop for coffee and cakes, fizz and crisps - the perfect finish to a family day out. But your dog is having none of it! You'd think she'd be worn out by now with all that tramping along cobbled streets, the run on the beach, splashing in the waves, clambering up stone steps, rolling in that dead fish …

Possibly it's because she's tired that she's being so difficult now. She won't settle - she's poking and pestering at hands and elbows, jogging your arm so your coffee sploshes on your lap. She's whining and pacing. She's begging for food. She doesn't seem to know how to switch off.

Does this picture look familiar? What can you do about this other than nagging, tutting, and keeping her on a tight lead?

There's a secret that a lot of family dog owners just don't know - and I'm going to explain its mysteries to you here.

We all seek security and a place to belong, a place where we can relax and feel at ease. As soon as we're in a strange place again, we get anxious and fidgety. Witness how long it takes people to choose a table in even an almost empty cafe!

A fretful toddler can halt her tears and become calm just by clutching her security blanket or beloved teddy bear close to her. Your dog is just the same. She needs to feel secure and safe in order to settle. She also needs to know that settling down is all she has to do right now.

Just before we start, let's have a look at some of the situations where this technique I'm going to teach you can help. Do they resonate with you? Does your dog do any of these things? One or two of them may be major annoyances for you. There may be others that are minor irritations that you didn't even know could be fixed!

- You've managed to infiltrate a visitor into your house and your dog will not leave them alone! Now your guest is giving you a stiff smile from behind a flurry of paws and tail, assuring you they don't mind - all the time wishing they hadn't come.

- You want to settle down for a picnic during a day out and your dog is trampling over the blanket, treading in the food, stealing the sandwiches … You can't relax and enjoy some quiet time with your family.

- You open the car door and your dog comes flying out to play an infuriating chase game around the car, leap up at a passing pensioner, or - tragically - run into the road.

- You're trying to help the children get their homework done while also organising their meal, but your dog continually interrupts proceedings by trying to steal the food you're making and disturbing the children. You've tried putting her in the garden, but she just barks and digs up the flowerbeds.

- You've had a nice family walk with your dog. You need to get everyone loaded back in the car with all their toys, bikes, and stuff. Your dog decides to play a game of Keep Away. She won't come to have her feet dried and get into the car.

- You're at the vets and your dog is straining on the lead, trying to get at the cat in its basket, jumping up at anyone who walks past, making you feel quite inadequate at being able to control her.

- Your dog never stops. She goes on and on and on. She doesn't rest - in fact, she seems to get more frantic, busy, and difficult as the day goes on. She totally resists the vital restorative sleep you know she needs.

- You find yourself thinking, "Whose idea was it to get a dog?"

Recognise any of these? They are all common events in many homes, and they really add up to a lot of frustration and annoyance. You chose to get a family dog because of the pleasure and richness she'd bring to your lives, but when your dog is driving you mad on a daily basis, you wonder how it's gone so wrong. That pleasure and richness can feel so far away.

It was having to learn the techniques to make a Brilliant Family Dog with my own busy household of multiple dogs, cats, sheep, goats, hens, and children that set me on the road to helping others do the same. I learnt early on that forcing someone to do something only resulted in grudging compliance at best; whereas getting them to participate and enjoy the process turned them into eager and fast learners. This applied equally to the dogs, the goats - and the children! The sheep and the cats not so much.

My qualifications range from the understanding of learning theory to specialist work for fearful, anxious, and growly dogs. Acquiring an anxious, growly dog of my own ensured that I learnt and understood the process of assimilating the dog into our world in a way which built her confidence.

There are some superb teachers and advocates of force-free dog training, and you'll find those I am particularly indebted to in the Resources section at the end of this book. Some of the methods I'll be showing you are well-known in the force-free dog training community, while many have my own particular twist.

My work revolves around puppies, new rescue dogs, growly dogs - and, of course, dog owners! There are many people more gifted than I who can train animals to do astonishing things. My gift lies in being able to convey my knowledge to the dog's caregiver in a way which has them saying, "It's so obvious when you put it like that!"

Dogs are individuals and so are their owners, so sometimes creativity and imagination are needed to solve a problem. There isn't a one-size-fits-all approach to training - as you'll see when you look at the Troubleshooting sections following each lesson in the book.

Here are some tips to keep in mind as you go through this book:

- Keep sessions very, very short - ten treats may be plenty long enough

- Keep treats flowing very fast whenever you're teaching anything new

- Remember that frustration and annoyance will not help anyone, so if things aren't going well in your (very short) session, just call it a day, have a game with your dog, and try again later.

- Move your training to different locations as you build up your dog's love of this game. First of all, just a different room in the house.

If you focus on this as a project - having just one short session a day - you'll be amazed how quickly you reach the stage of being able to use your new skills anywhere, any time.

Follow the steps that I outline for you. Don't skip or jump ahead. Work on each step till it's more or less right, then move on. There's no need to be a perfectionist here. You don't want to get stuck.

I suggest you read the whole book before you start so you yourself are clear about what you need and what you are aiming for. Then re-read the lesson you're working on and go straight into your very short session. After this you can assess where you are and check the Troubleshooting section for any difficulties that are relevant to you and your dog. Then you'll be ready for your next session the next day.

Just one skill is needed

You may be surprised to learn that all the pictures I painted before (and many more) can be completely resolved by one simple technique. You teach your dog to LOVE her mat - her security blanket - a place to find comfort and freedom from anxiety. Once she does, she will become putty in your hands.

And no! It's not difficult to teach. Even young puppies in an exciting environment can learn this invaluable skill quickly.

Puppies from 16-20 weeks resting quietly on their mats before Puppy Class begins

Dogs are doers

They can't exist in a vacuum. They need to be doing something. Teaching your dog to keep her mat on the floor by lying on top of it is the perfect solution to relieving anxiety and stress.

All you need is a small mat and a bit of teaching to make your dog feel secure and at home, even when she's out. She'll have a place she can rest and relax without worrying about where she is or what she should be doing.

In this book, I'll show you how to get your dog manic about her mat. As soon as you put it down she will hurl herself onto it as if it might float away and escape if she's not fast enough! She will stay firmly on her mat, anchoring it to the floor, and she will even stay there regardless of how many crumbs the children drop, until you are ready to release her.

The magical aspects of the mat are that it:

- Acts like a toddler's security blanket, making your dog feel comfortable and at ease
- Creates a bubble for the dog to stay in safely while she observes the world, dispelling the anxiety she might otherwise feel
- Builds a state of relaxation which becomes connected with the mat; i.e. dog on mat = snoozing dog
- Is especially valuable with reactive or anxious dogs; they don't have to be on guard duty the whole time
- Keeps your dog content and amused when coupled with treats or a food-toy
- Your dog thinks, "I know what I should be doing," as she settles down

Are you ready to get started? Let's go!

Chapter 1
Introducing the Mat!

Cricket is watching with interest as this strange new mat floats down to the ground

So let's get cracking.

There are some things you're going to need to ensure success with these lessons, so I'll introduce them to you now.

What do you need?

Your Mat

You will only use this mat for relax and settle work. After every training session, put it away. (I'll explain why in a minute.) So you don't want to use your dog's bed. You also won't have much success with a towel or blanket - they'll get screwed up and in a mess in no time. Something flat, small, and reasonably stiff will fit the bill.

An ideal mat is a soft doormat with nonslip backing (inexpensive), or you can use a carpet sample (often free) from a carpet shop. These are usually neatly bound all around the edge.

As far as size goes, you want a mat that's big enough for the dog to sit on but not much bigger. Remember it's not a bed, so she doesn't have to fit completely on the mat. That's probably a relief to hear if you have a Deerhound or a Pyrenean Mountain Dog! The smaller the mat is, the easier it'll be to carry around with you when you are out.

Treats

The treats need to be very tasty - your dog has got to really want them! You don't want her chewing and chomping on a biscuit for so long that she forgets what she earned it for! The treat needs to slip down quickly and make your dog think, "Wow! How can I get some more of that?" Your dog needs to know what you like and what does not cut it with you. So every time she does something you like, you can mark it by saying, "YES!" and giving her a treat.

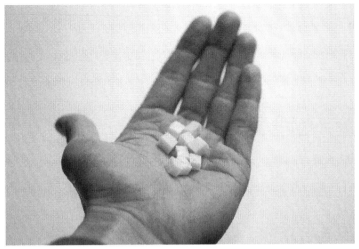

Small, tasty, treats!

Good treats

- Cheese
- Sausage
- Ham
- Chicken
- Frankfurter
- Salami
- Homemade sardine, tuna, or ham cookies
- Freeze-dried 100% meat treats
- Dehydrated liver, heart, lung, etc

…real food in other words. Ideally, they slip down quickly so your dog wants more. Cut them up small - just pea-size will do nicely.

OK treats

- High-quality grain-free commercial treats

Fairly rubbish treats

- Your dog's usual kibble (She gets it anyway. Why should she have to work for it?)
- Cat biscuits
- Dog biscuits
- Stuff of unrecognisable composition sold as pet treats
- Anything you wouldn't put in your own mouth

Do you work more enthusiastically for £60 an hour or for 50p an hour? Quite so. Your dog is the same. Be sure the treats you're offering are worth working for!

Troubleshooting

Why do I have to keep giving my dog treats? Shouldn't she do what she's told anyway?

I only give my dogs a treat when they've done something I like. I aim to get through a lot of treats every day! Treats are not a moral issue. They are a means to an end. The end is your dog calmly relaxing on her mat. If employing a few bits of cheese means that my outings are enjoyable and my visitors unmolested then that's a good deal to me.

But isn't all this extra food bad for him?

You're using high-quality food for treats. It's not like giving chocolate to a child. You have to feed your dog anyway, so you may as well get some mileage from it. If your dog is overweight, simply remove an equivalent amount of food from his dinner.

Your sessions will be really short - a minute or two at the most - so you'll only need about 20-30 little treats. Later on in your training, you could use your dog's dinner, fed morsel by morsel.

Chapter 2
Starting with the Mat

The treat goes right on the mat, between your dog's paws

Read this chapter through to the end before getting started with your dog - you want to make sure it's fresh in your mind. In fact, leave this page open so you can quickly refer to it if you lose the thread.

Have several treats ready in your hand for quick-fire delivery.

Lesson 1
Front paws on the Mat

1. Call your dog over and give her a treat to show her that something interesting is going on.

2. Now, with a flourish, produce your lovely new mat from behind your back and float it to the floor in front of her nose.

3. When she looks at the mat, immediately place a treat on it. This first treat is a reward for your dog interacting with the mat simply by looking at it.

4. As she steps onto the mat to get that treat - bang! - place a treat between her paws on the mat. While she's eating that treat, if she still has her paws on the mat, she gets another, and another. The treats should flow very fast. A good rate of delivery is one every two seconds. Your dog is being rewarded simply for having her front paws on the mat. *Note: Each treat goes on the mat between her paws. All you want to focus on in this lesson is Front Paws on the Mat. Everything else your dog learns will follow from this step.*

5. After giving her three or four treats, pause for two seconds (just two seconds - no more!) to see what she does. Your dog will probably do one of these three things:

   a. She'll stay exactly where she is. Excellent! Reward her with three more quick treats.

   b. She wanders off. *Wait.* Stand by the mat to give her time to realise that you still have good treats to be eaten. If she seems to have lost the plot, you can move round the mat to make sure it's between her and you - if necessary make a kissy noise to get her attention back. She'll most likely wander back and by accident or design she'll put her front feet on the mat. Hooray! You're back in business. Give her three or four treats between the paws, just as before.

c. She looks at you in puzzlement, wondering why you've stopped dishing out the treats. She may jump up on you: stand still and ignore her entirely. She may bark at you: look away and ignore her entirely. She may paddle her feet: wait. And she may sit: Jackpot! - give her three or four very quick treats on the mat between her paws!

Sooner or later, in this first quick session, your dog will sit. If that doesn't happen, simply repeat Steps 3 and 4 until she does sit. Just front paws on the mat no longer pays. You've moved the goalposts: *she now needs to sit with front paws on the mat.*

This is your new criterion. Sitting on the mat is what now pays, and nowhere have you told your dog to do anything!

To end your minute-long session, toss a treat away from the mat, and then pick up the mat when the dog is off it.

She's worked hard! So have a game with her with a toy.

You need to repeat this very short session several times, over several days, until when you get your mat out you have difficulty getting it to the floor because your dog is trying to leap onto it! Without telling her to do anything, she's learnt that the mat is a great place to be. Standing on it is good, and sitting on it is even more productive.

One thing I hope you've noticed during this first stage is how your dog stops dancing around, gazes at you questioningly, and *thinks*. You can see the wheels turning while she tries to solve this new puzzle you've set her. She slows down and makes thoughtful responses.

You may find that she is very tired after a couple of minutes of playing this new game. She's been thinking hard, and thinking is hard work. Encourage her to rest and let her brain file away what she's just learnt.

Troubleshooting

My dog has no interest in the mat!

At your next session, get her playing with you first. If it doesn't get her over-excited, you could run round the room with her or play with a toy. You can ramp up the energy and excitement. This should make her interested in what you're doing with this mat-thing.

Another method to try is to throw a treat on the floor for her to grab, then another the opposite way. Then slap your mat down right in her path. Be very quick to put the treat on it where she's looking. Work fast!

My dog is too distracted to look at the mat.

Choose a time when he's more likely to pay attention to you and your good food. Wait till the children are occupied quietly in another room. Maybe before his dinner, when the household is quiet, when he's not too tired, and when he's hungry. Make sure you have treats that he finds very exciting.

When I put the mat on the floor, my dog steps on it, then gets off again, and looks worried.

First, it's great that she steps on it! It's possible you aren't being quick enough with your treat. While you're standing and holding the mat, get your brain in gear, ensure you have a treat in your other hand and that your dog is paying attention to what's about to happen. Then whack down your mat and shoot your treat down between her paws as soon as she even looks at the mat. Then another and another. Do not miss her first response! We are teaching our dog to think and experiment. Your dog thought she should put her feet on the mat, but you were too slow to reward her so she thought she had made a mistake. So she backed off, and looked worried wondering what she should do.

If it helps, rehearse the steps by yourself beforehand when she isn't in the room.

She sits or stands beside the mat, but she won't get on it.

Be sure to place the treat - quickly - on the mat as soon as she looks at it. If the mat is small and the dog large, put the treat on the far side of the mat so there's a good chance she'll step on it, so you can reward Front Paws on the Mat.

He actually treats the mat as a force field and avoids stepping on it!

It's possible the mat may have some unpleasant scent on it that is putting him off. Try using other flat things and textures to see what he's happy to step on. If he likes lying on his bed or a sunny spot in the room, trying putting the mat there just to help him get started.

She stands on the mat alright, but when she sits, she moves backwards so her paws move off the mat.

Good girl! She's trying hard to do what you want! Encourage her to move a little further forward on the mat by placing the treats in front of her paws instead of between them, then when she sits she should still keep her feet on the mat. If she always paddles backwards when she sits, you could do a separate session or two practicing sits with her back to a wall. This will keep her from moving backwards, which is a habit she has formed at some point, and she'll learn to sit straight away,

My floor is all carpeted. How can she tell when she's on the mat?

Good question! Dogs' paws are very sensitive, but if the mat you've chosen feels exactly the same as your carpet in texture, simply flip the mat over. Working with the mat the wrong way up, she'll get the rough side (if carpet sample) or rubber backing (if a mat), and will clearly feel the difference in surface.

He sits on the mat, but hops up again.

When you put the treat between their paws for sitting, a few dogs will hop up again and stand to eat the treat. In this case, as soon as he sits feed his treat to his mouth (then another, then another) rather than putting them on the mat. If he hops up, stop the treat flow. He'll soon get the message that treats come only when he's sitting.

My dog is looking quite anxious about all this.

Give her a break and try again later. Make sure your sessions are short. I would suggest two minutes max. Ensure that you have good treats that she really wants (skip the biscuits - use proper food), and be very generous with your speed. One treat every two seconds is a good rate.

I thought we were doing ok then she stood and barked at me!

You probably have a quick dog who thinks you aren't going fast enough! Or maybe she's a bit confused about what she's meant to do and she's barking out of frustration. Toss a treat off the mat for her and just start again from the beginning. Be quick with giving her a treat, and get it to her before she draws breath to bark. You can quickly separate the bark from the "being on the mat," then you can carry on.

I have to wave a treat in front of him to get him to come to the mat.

This is called luring, and while luring has its place in dog training, its place is not here! We're not trying to coax him onto the mat. If you need food to get your dog to come to you, two things can go wrong.

First, you are giving him a choice. Giving him a choice is good only as long as you don't lose out! You are asking him, "Do you want to stay where you are, or do you want this treat?"

What do you do if he decides to stay where he is?

Second, if you have to show him the colour of your money before you ask for anything, he'll soon learn that if you don't have food you are powerless and not worth bothering with.

As if those two things aren't bad enough, there's also the fact that he won't be choosing to go on the mat - he'll just be following his nose for the treat in front of it and he'll have no idea where he's going at all! This is just like when we drive following another car. We're so concerned with keeping the car in our sights that we have little idea where we actually are and are none the wiser about our route when we arrive at our destination. It's essential that your dog chooses to go on the mat, by himself. Choice is very important in all of these lessons!

In this Chapter we have established that:

- The mat is a touchpad. When your dog's paws are on it, treats magically appear between them
- Doing something new brings rewards. She doesn't have to wait to be told to do something
- Doing something different brings more rewards. We're building an enquiring mind here
- Working very quickly is essential to keep the flow
- "I can think for myself!" she says as she hops onto the mat and claims her reward!

Chapter 3
Mat Magic!

Bailey (15 weeks) relaxes at Puppy Class

So now, when you bring out the mat and swoosh it to the floor, your dog leaps straight on it. Let's move on to some more mat magic!

Your dog clearly understands that sitting on the mat results in good things. The next stage is to get her to lie down on the mat.

In the same way that we haven't yet told the dog to do anything at all - we've just waited for her to make good choices that she finds pay - we won't be telling her to sit or lie down either. You probably got her sitting on the mat in the last few sessions. If not, just continue the very short mat sessions till she gets it. When she eventually lowers herself into a sit - throw a party! Cheer, dance, throw treats, and then end the session.

We've moved the goalposts once - so that the dog is now being paid for sitting - and now we're going to move them again.

Lesson 2
Down on the Mat

After a few speedy sits and treats from Lesson 1, you can now expect your dog to lie down.

1. Simply break your rhythm and pause in the same way as you did to achieve a Sit.

    a. Your dog may wiggle her bottom or paddle her feet to check she's sitting already: wait. She may try a different place on the mat: ignore what you don't want and keep waiting. If she seems anxious, go back to rewarding her for sitting, then try again a little later. You don't need to maintain a stony silence! Some encouraging noises are good so she doesn't get worried and give up, but at all costs resist the temptation to tell her what to do!

    b. She may bark or poke you to say, "Hey, I'm sitting!" Ignore these actions and wait. Wait for a good decision from her.

    c. She may move a front paw forward while she considers changing position, YES! treat, treat, treat between the paws! You don't need to wait for a full Down – just a slight move in the right direction is rewardable. She will probably complete the down action to get at the treats. Stop the treat flow as soon as she sits up again.

2. Repeat this stage several times over the next few days to establish that the default position on the mat now is to lie down.

Keep your sessions very short. Kettle time is always a good opportunity for a quick training session. While you wait for the kettle to boil, grab a small handful of tasty treats, toss the mat on the floor and you're off!

How do I get my dog to lie down?

By this stage, your dog will be flying to her mat and landing on it in a down position. Just sometimes, though, especially with very small dogs, they don't get that they need to move on from a sit to a down position - or they lie the front half down and the tail end pops up into the air! If your dog is not lying down there are a few things we can do to teach her. The first one you can do on the mat, the others anywhere.

Teaching her Down on the mat

1. When you place the food between her paws, keep your hand over it so she has to get her head down and burrow in under your hand to reach the treat. Quite soon she'll need to move a front paw forward to help her bend - Yes! Treat! Next time you can wait till the paw moves a little further forward and her elbow touches the mat - Yes! Treat!

2. Repeat this till you have both elbows on the mat, then treat, treat, treat, break, and have a game.

You don't have to wait for a complete Down to reward and encourage her - just a tiny move in the direction of a Down will do.

Capture a Down

1. Choose a time when you can relax and your puppy is playing with her toys.

2. Keep an eye on her and when she eventually lies down, say "Yes!" and ask her to come over for a treat. She won't know why she's being rewarded yet, but that doesn't matter. After a while she'll lie down again - "Yes!" - she gets up and comes over to you for another treat. Let her wander off again. To begin with these events may be ten minutes apart.

3. Watch carefully, as at some stage your puppy will twig what's happening and tentatively slide a paw forward and start to lower herself to the floor: "Yes!!" Party! She's got it!

4. Now you can start adding the word "Down." Only say it once, just as she's about to lie down. In one short session you have a puppy who will lie down when you ask.

Lie down in a tunnel

The tunnel can be furniture - a chair cross-bar just the right height for your dog to lie under may work well - or your legs.

1. Sit on the floor with your legs stretched out in front of you.

2. Raise your knees and make a big tunnel.

3. With your dog on your left, put your right hand loaded with a treat under your knees and draw her through, giving her the treat as she emerges the other side.

4. After running her through the tunnel a couple of times she will learn it's a game and not a trap. Now repeat it, but lower your knees slightly so she has to crawl through.

5. As soon as her bum goes to the floor you can release your treat. Once this is happening every time you can label this action of hers as "Down".

Luring

1. Put the treat to her nose so that her nose is touching your hand.

2. Lower your hand slowly, keeping the nose attached. Move it slightly down and into the dog so that it takes her nose down between her paws.

3. Give her a treat.

4. Next one, wait for the front legs to bend a little so the elbows come down.

5. Give her a treat. And so on.

6. Once the elbows are fully on the floor, her bottom will collapse down.

Occasionally a dog will remain in a play-bow and resolutely refuse to lower her rear end. Worry not! Just give this a suitable name like "Take a bow" just as she's doing it, and you now have a cute trick. Try one of the other methods to achieve your Down.

Luring can work, but you must stop offering food in the hand that was holding it as soon as she's got the idea. You still reward your dog with a treat for doing what you want, but after she's done it, not before.

Troubleshooting

My dog will lie down on the mat, but she bounces straight back up again!

That sounds as if she's got the idea to lie down but she doesn't realise she needs to stay down. You're obviously doing very well so far. Have a few treats ready in your hand. Don't use a pot or bag as you want to be able to react as soon as she even starts to move into a down position. Once she lies down, you can start shovelling the treats into her mouth, one, two, three … As long as she's down you keep posting the treats in. As soon as she lifts up the treats stop again.

My dog is off and on the mat the whole time.

If your dog is on the mat, off the mat, back on the mat to get a treat, off again, back on for a treat, etc, you're building a chain of actions that you don't want! If he leaves the mat then comes back - it's not bad or wrong, it's just not going to earn a treat. So when he steps back on, tell him how good he is, wait for a second or so, then reward him. He'll soon learn stepping off the mat delays the rewards and opt to stay put.

I've got her to lie down by luring her. How do I stop having to move her down with the treat?

Nice work! When you use a lure to get your dog to do something, it's essential that you stop luring as soon as possible. See the last Troubleshooting Question and Answer in Chapter 2: Starting with the Mat, which explains it fully. Instead, wait and let your dog work it out.

I put the mat on the floor and my dog says, "So?"

If your dog is not interested in the mat, it means you haven't built up a strong enough association that Mat = Good Things. Go back to the beginning - you can run through this very quickly - and be sure that first your dog is hungry and not too tired, second the environment is quiet, calm, and not distracting, and - most important! - you're using small treats that he thinks are *divine*.

We've taught the dog to love getting on to her mat. The next step is to teach how to get *off* the mat. She can't just get up and mosey off when she feels like it. Once she's on the mat, she has to stay there till you release her.

Lesson 3
Learning when to get off the mat

You have just rewarded your dog quickly several times in a row for lying down on her mat.

1. Keeping the same rhythm, and without moving away from the mat, hold your hand out with a treat at dog-nose level a yard or so from the mat and say, "Break." Your dog will bounce off the mat to sniff your hand and eat the treat. Now stand up and *wait*. What's going to happen next?

a. If you've kept the rhythm going there's a high chance that your dog will bounce straight back on to her mat. Yes! Treat! Wait for her to lie down - more treats!

b. She bounces off the mat for her treat in your hand, then she stops, unsure what to do next. *Wait*. Let her work it out. Chances are she'll suddenly remember where she was getting all those rewards and step back onto her mat. If she seems anxious, make encouraging noises till she at least looks at the mat - Yes! Treat on the mat! We're off again.

c. She wanders off to see if there are more treats on the ground. If you have any idea this may happen, practice with a long lead on the dog and your foot on the end of it. This will limit her wanderings to the area near the mat. *Wait* and change your position if necessary so you are the opposite side of the mat from her. At some stage she is going to wander back towards you and accidentally put her paws on the mat - Yes! Treat! Now we're back in business.

2. Practice breaks now and then, but most of the treats your dog gets should still be between the paws on the mat. At least six rewards for lying down on the mat before you do another break. We want the association with the mat to be lying down and keeping still, not bouncing on and off!

From now on, whenever you want your dog off the mat - and certainly at the end of the short session - you can "break" her. Don't forget to have a quick game with her - she's worked hard for you.

As you continue with these sessions you'll find that your dog is happy to wait till she hears her release word. All she has to do is stay there and wait for the rewards to trickle in. She's quite clear in what she needs to do.

I was working with my dog Lacy while making coffee one day. She was lying nicely on her mat and getting rewarded from time to time. Suddenly there was a hullabaloo from the garden - the hens were squawking, and the other dogs flew out to see what was going on. We had a visiting dog, and I thought he may have been upsetting the hens, so I raced out too. It was just a couple of hens having an argument - the visiting dog was innocent. Everyone calmed down. When I strolled back in to get my coffee, there was Lacy, lying still on her mat amidst all the kerfuffle and excitement! Yes, I'd entirely forgotten her in the moment. But what a good girl!

That's the power of teaching your dog to stay on the mat until told otherwise. She was quite clear that what she was doing was keeping that mat still under her.

Troubleshooting

Do I have to use the word "break"?

You can use absolutely any word you like! I'd avoid "okay" because we say that a million times a day and this can lead to confusion. You want a word which only means "you're released from the thing I asked you to do." Make it crystal clear. When I say, "Break," my dogs don't run away from the mat, they run over to me to see what's next.

Just when it seems to be going well, she wanders off the mat.

I'd guess that you've slowed down a bit with the treats, so perhaps she thinks you've finished. In the first place, keep up a steady flow of treats when she's doing what you want. Practice your break so she's quite clear when she can move off. Keep your sessions very short!

My dog keeps licking her lips. Does this mean she likes the treats a lot? She's quite shy at the best of times.

Lip-licking, along with yawning when not tired, avoiding eye contact, looking away - among other gestures - is what's known as a calming signal. These are easily read by other, socially-skilled, dogs, but not so well read by us dog owners! It's a sign of slight anxiety. She's worried she's doing the wrong thing.

Whenever a dog is anxious, the best thing is to back off or ease up a little. Bring some more joy and lightness to your sessions. Keep them incredibly short (maybe 6 treats), and be sure to play with your dog as a big reward after!

She takes ages to come back on the mat and goes off sniffing instead.

She seems distracted. The treats should be so delicious that she can't wait to get back on the mat to get another. Make sure the floor is clear of toys and crumbs or other small distractions. Be sure the environment is not distracting - the children playing noisily outside for instance - and put her on a six-foot lead which you can put your foot on so she can't go wandering off.

All these treats! Do I have to give them forever?

That's such a good question! Treats - in fact anything the dog finds pleasurable - are invaluable for teaching the dog something new. Look at it this way: you've got to feed your dog anyway, so why not get some mileage from the food? If you put all the food in a bowl, put it down and walk away, you are missing a huge learning opportunity for your dog! As you become skilled as a trainer, you'll know when to speed up and when to slow down the number of treats. You'll also learn to vary the type of rewards you use. We'll look at this in more detail later on. For now, just keep dishing out the rewards whenever your dog does something you like. You'll be able to cut the treats right down later - but not yet. Don't push the scaffolding away too soon!

In this Chapter we have established that:

- The mat represents a very special place in your dog's eyes
- It pleases you enormously when she puts her paws on it
- She looks forward to you getting the mat out as it's a guaranteed way to get rewards
- Your dog needs to anchor the mat to the floor so the rewards can keep coming
- Helping your dog will actually slow down her rate of learning
- "I can make good decisions!"

Chapter 4
What do I do with this mat now?

Lacy relaxes on her mat while I enjoy coffee and a good book

Let's look now at what you can do next. You have taught your dog a game with the mat which she looks forward to and engages in with enthusiasm. You have built this up in stages with clarity. Now we can take it on the road!

Coffee with a friend, or Sunday lunch at the pub

Now you've got this working smoothly at home, start taking it out of the house to new places. Keep your first trip fairly short. Start by going to a place you already know.

Let's say you're meeting a friend at a café. There are plenty of good cafés that will allow dogs - many welcome them. The same goes for pubs. In fact you'll find internet resources that list dog-friendly eateries. I have a printout of dog-friendly venues for my locality that I keep in the car. If I want to stop somewhere for a meal or a break, I can go straight to a suitable café or hostelry, without having to go in first and ask if I may bring the dog in.

Even those who don't want dogs inside are usually happy for you to sit at an outside table with your dog.

Treat your dog just as you would a toddler, and set out on your journey well-equipped. Bring her mat, really good treats, chews, a filled food toy, a favourite teddy bear … Be sure you have plenty of things to distract her with. It will really help if your friend is willing to allow you to focus on your dog whenever necessary.

1. Give her a run or an exciting game beforehand so she's ready to settle down.

2. Choose a spot to place the mat where your dog won't get trodden on. Avoid high traffic areas, such as near the main door, the toilets, and the kitchens. These places are too busy.

3. Then simply reward your dog with good things as soon as she puts herself on the mat. You'll have her on a lead, of course, but make sure it's loose enough for her to be able to find a comfortable position, while you have the handle firmly in your hand.

Never tie your dog to a table or chair - that's far too risky. Just have the lead on your wrist then you'll be aware straight away if she's getting agitated for any reason. Maybe when your dog is as experienced as Lacy is, you can attach the lead to a suitable fixed point - like a very heavy chair.

On this first occasion you may spend more time making sure your dog is content than chatting to your friend. But this is insurance! Next time will be much easier. Once your first trip has been successful, you can try different places. Soon your dog will be able to go anywhere with you - settling down and amusing herself without annoying you or anybody else. This is one good reason for having a small, easily transportable mat. Once your Mat Magic is well-established, anything will do for a mat.

My son and I were out walking and found a pub showing a cricket match on tv, so in we went to have a quick lunch. Sky the Whippet was with us. She was tired, but the floors were hard, and - as you may know - thin-skinned whippets love their comfort! She really wanted to lie down, but did not want to rest on floorboards. You could as well have asked her to lie down on a bed of nails. It was a hot summer's day, so we had no jumpers or coats we could put down for her. We were miles from the car and this was an unplanned stop so we had not brought Sky's mat. I took one of the flimsy paper serviettes provided with our meal, opened it out and put it on the floor. With relief, Sky lay straight down on it and rested.

A peaceful evening in the living room

Probably the first and easiest way most people will use their mat is to encourage their dog to settle in the living room of an evening. If your dog has been accustomed to jumping around and pestering you whenever you take to your armchair, you will love this! If your dog already has a bed in the living room, then you can transfer to that after you've established the new setup, but begin with the mat.

1. Be sure your dog has had a good game in the garden or that she's had a walk. She needs something to puff her out before you ask her to settle down.

2. Sit in your chair, put the mat on the floor beside you, and place the reward between her paws as usual. This time you can use your dog's dinner. Feed one morsel at a time. You can also use treats, but use fairly boring ones, like her kibble.

3. As you both settle for the evening, you'll find your rate of reward naturally slowing down.

4. Don't forget to "break" your dog when you've had enough. She can leave her mat if she wants to, or she can stay zizzing. "Break" just means you have released her from the session and she can do what she wants.

To begin with, do this just for a few minutes. After a few sessions, over a few days, you can start working a bit longer. You can have chews or food toys to keep her occupied then.

Incidentally, to add a vocal cue for the mat, just say "Mat," "Bed," "Chill," "Settle" - whatever you want - quietly, exactly as your dog is stepping onto the mat. You're describing her action. That's how dogs make the connection between the word and the deed. They don't have verbal language like we do, but they can associate a sound with an action (think doorbell). After doing this for a while, you can say your cue just as she's thinking about going on the mat.

One golden advantage of my dogs being happy to go on their mats is this: if my four dogs are pacing or playing in the living room when I want some peace and quiet, I just say, "Bed!" and they all go straight to the nearest bed and lie down. There is such a strong history of reward from parking themselves on something – be it a mat, a stool, or a garden chair – that they don't see it as a punishment.

Dogs need a huge amount of sleep, so as long as they've had entertainment and activity in the day there's no need for them to keep going all evening. Indeed, keeping going is a bad idea, because they will get ragged, frustrated, and difficult. Value sleep!

Visiting the vet

Your dog will have to visit the vet from time to time. She's already experienced a trip to the vet, and she'll already have an opinion about it.

If you've developed a good relationship with your vet and staff, your dog may eagerly bounce into the waiting room - seeing it as a purely social visit. Some dogs though, may have had to undergo painful procedures or have had poor experiences with other dogs in the waiting room while awaiting their turn. If this is the case with your dog, you may need to rebuild her confidence.

The smell of the vet's clinic is very strong and particular to that place. Just walking to the door, your dog will know where she is. When you think of ice cream, maybe it triggers your earliest memories - connecting it to the seaside or a childhood visit to Granny's. Tastes and smells can evoke very strong feelings. The dog's taste and smell mechanisms are thousands of times more powerful than ours! So we want to make sure that strong smell of the vet's is associated with not only good experiences but also a state of calm and relaxation. So whether your dog is a social butterfly or is anxious - wide-eyed and panting - at the vet's, the foundation you've built with your mat will greatly contribute to this calm and relaxed state.

By the way, my dogs are encouraged to acknowledge people when they're in the vet's waiting room, but I don't let them interact with any other animals that may be there. Why are those animals there? Well, they could be sick, they could be contagious, they could be flea-ridden, they could be in pain. Not a good basis for meeting another dog. Keeping your dog to yourself is a very important piece of etiquette for vet visits.

Take your mat with you, along with a few other things to amuse your dog if you anticipate a long wait. Put the mat on the floor beside you. On goes your dog, and assuming the vet visit will not entail anaesthetic (so eating beforehand is ok), on go your treats. Quite soon you have a contented happy dog who is not anxiously scanning the room to see who may be coming in next.

Other clients will more than likely admire what you are doing and try to get their dog to calm a little too. Sadly, they won't have your Magic Mat Recipe, so they'll probably employ a lot of lead-yanking, nagging, and complaining, which won't get them very far.

When it's time to go in to see the vet, you can "break" your dog off the mat and take it with you into the examination room. While you are talking to the vet your dog can be lying on her mat at your feet - rather than lurching and pulling on the lead, trying to stick her nose in the sharps bin and so on. You will be maintaining the calm and relaxed state the mat induced out in the waiting room. When it's time, you can break your dog off the mat, lift her onto the table and carry on treating her for staying still while she is examined and assessed by the vet.

Not only will you be bursting with pride that your dog is so well behaved in a potentially stressful situation, but others will notice too.

Amanda and Harley, her labradoodle pup and one of my Puppy Class students - proudly told me about her puppy's vet visit. She found the waiting room very busy, with dogs whining. Harley lay quietly on his mat chewing a chewtoy. No-one could believe that he was only five months old and so calm and well-behaved.

"That mat is going everywhere with us from now on!" Amanda said.

Harley (20 weeks) in the vet's waiting room, showing how it's done

Seeing is believing. You have to try things to find out just how well they work. Amanda believes in her mat!

By the way - if you don't have any vet visits scheduled, you can always drop in at a time when they're not too busy, greet the receptionist, and do a little mat practice in the waiting room. Vet staff are usually very pleased at anything owners do to keep their pet calm on a visit. It's no fun for them to wrestle with a distressed dog when they're trying to help. So they will be happy for you to do this - if a little bemused!

Family picnic

You've probably been somewhere new and exciting - the beach, a forest, open fields - and the children and your family dog have played themselves to a standstill.

Time for the picnic.

While you spread out the food on the cloth or table, put out the cushions or chairs, and settle down to eat, you don't want to have to be on edge the whole time wondering where on earth your dog has gone. For those of you with foodaholic dogs, you don't want their eyes and nose following every morsel you put in your mouth.

Put the mat on the ground near you, but just far enough away that she won't be tempted to snaffle your sandwiches. Have her on a loose lead as well, but the mat will telling her to stay put. Occasional treats may help, but a food-filled toy will certainly focus her mind on staying where she is until she dozes off.

Once the children have refuelled, you can break her off the mat so you can all carry on the games. Meanwhile she's had a good rest - hopefully a sleep too, and is ready for more play without getting ragged and over-excited.

In this Chapter we have learnt that:

- The mat can go with you anywhere
- It is a safe haven
- It becomes self-rewarding - you can slow the treats right down
- You can all relax
- "I can enjoy being out with the family without bouncing all the time!"

Chapter 5
Taking it on the road

Coco waits on his mat while I answer the doorbell

Let's explore now all the ways your mat can help you in your daily life with your family dog. Once you've established the mat as a safe place for her to park herself - for as long as you want her parked - the way is opened for you to use it in many different interactions with your dog. It becomes a normal part of the dog's response. Instead of leaping and bounding around aimlessly, she'll know that putting herself on her mat is a wise choice and may well earn her rewards.

How about a situation which is a big problem for many dog-owners? A ring at the doorbell.

The doorbell!

The doorbell can send many dogs into a state of extreme excitement which makes them very hard to control. You may grab your dog by the collar to try to answer the door with your arm being yanked up and down by a demented dog. You may just open the door a crack because your dog is fearful of strangers and may decide to "have a go." Perhaps you just resort to shutting her in another room.

How about this instead?

1. Teach your dog that when the doorbell rings, she runs to her mat and will be rewarded mightily for that. This may take you a week or two. If you focus on it for a week you may be amazed how good she gets! You do it when there aren't any real visitors, just you and her, and perhaps a useful third person to stay outside and ring the bell periodically. You are simply teaching her that the sound of the doorbell is the signal for her to race to her mat, lie down, and stay there for the flow of rewards.

2. Once you've got this stage down, you may set things up so you can stay by your dog, feeding her treats, while someone else answers the door. Keep it all very brief and good fun.

3. Now when the doorbell rings, your dog will go to her mat and wait patiently for the treats to start appearing. If you're a good shot and the mat is well positioned in sight of the door, you can buzz treats to her while you speak to your caller. This will gradually become her default behaviour on hearing the bell.

If this is a major and well-established problem at your home, there are a couple of gadgets that can help you with this.

For the training: A wireless doorbell (very cheap). You can place the amplifier wherever you want, stand right by the mat, and just hold the button in your hand and press it. This allows you to be right on top of the situation. As soon as the doorbell rings your dog hops on her mat and you can post the treats into your dog without delay.

For the real thing: A Manners Minder or Treat'n'Train (not so cheap). This is a remote controlled device that administers treats either as you press the remote button or on a set schedule of your choosing. This is especially useful if your dog is fearful and anxious about visitors. She'll be paying attention to the dispensing machine and not worrying about the person at the door. At my house, once the machine is switched on, my anxious dog Lacy stays rivetted in front of it, her nose hovering over the dispenser tray, despite the two-headed monsters at the door!

Targets

Not the sort you have to achieve at work, more the archery sort with a bull's eye. The mat is what's known technically as a "target behaviour." That is to say, the dog is targetting the mat with her front feet. As we've seen, this leads to a Down and ultimately a relaxed state.

You can transfer this targetting to any object you like: another bed in the house, your lap (for very small dogs!), a footstool, in the back of the car where your dog travels, your jumper on the floor (for when you forget your mat, like I did with Sky the Whippet), and so on.

Your dog has learnt to stay on the mat till you release her with "Break".

So how about this for calm exits from the house?

1. Strategically place your mat a couple of yards in front of the door.

2. Put the lead on your dog and walk towards the door.

3. She should see the mat and sit or lie down on it without needing to be told, but she may be excited that you're going for a walk and you may need to remind her.

4. Put your hand on the door handle and if necessary ask her to sit.

5. Open the door a crack, shut it again, say, "break," and toss a treat away behind her so she gets up to eat the treat, then comes back to her mat and sits as you put your hand on the handle again.

6. Keep going with short sessions, opening the door a little more each time until you're able to open the door fully without her shifting from her mat.

7. Open the door wide, pause for a moment, then break her to step outside with you. No mad crashing the door and yanking your arm. If the prospect of the walk is too exciting for your dog to focus, start by using an inner door - a bedroom door or some other non-exciting doorway.

And this one, for the car?

1. Your dog is in your car, restrained of course, either in a crate or with a harness and lead.

2. You open the car door. Dog sits patiently.

3. You open the crate door, reach in and attach the lead, or switch the car restraint for your walking lead. Dog continues to sit patiently.

4. Now, when the coast is clear and the road safe, you can give your release word, "Break."

5. Out hops your dog.

6. If you really want to make this perfect and dazzle everyone watching, you can have her mat ready on the ground so she immediately parks herself on that mat and sits waiting - still patiently - for you to shut the door, lock the car, and start on your walk. You'll be able to skip the second mat once this is a habit.

Preparing dinner

This is one use of the Magic Mat that I absolutely love. There are few things more annoying than trying to cook dinner while your dog gets under your feet to trip you up (very dangerous too with hot pans involved), or finding your elbow continually nudged by a searching nose, or worst of all, turning to get a knife to cut the meat, then turning back to find the meat gone. All this can be solved with your mat!

1. Choose a convenient place for the mat. I suggest somewhere out of your way but close enough that your dog can still see you.

2. Load a food toy with goodies (possibly your dog's dinner), and prepare your meal without help from your four-footed, begging friend.

3. Always remember to break your dog when she's allowed off her mat. If she comes off without permission, I would just stand still, say "Where are you meant to be?" and wait for her to return. Once she puts herself back on the mat you can tell her how clever she is and carry on as before. Like us, dogs take pride in working out puzzles and doing something they know to be right.

Mat substitutes

One of the great benefits of teaching your dog to love her mat is that you can transfer what she does on the mat to any other object you name a "mat".

You can use a doormat, a low wall, a barrel, a box, a mounting-block, a boulder, a tree stump, a chair, a picnic table, a step, a raised bed, an armchair, or - as in the case of Sky the Whippet - a paper square! Really, you can use anything that has a defined edge or border.

After a 5-mile walk with my gang we stopped at a café. No, I was not going to carry four mats in my backpack! I knew I'd find something suitable to ground them for a few minutes. Sure enough, there was an umbrella over the table outside the café. It had a large weighted base a few inches high - just big enough to accommodate four tired dogs!

You can usually find something to make into an honorary mat, wherever you go.

Reports from the Front Line

Here are some comments from students in my puppy classes, where matwork with all its applications is an important component:

"Here is Samson being as good as gold in the pub this afternoon after Puppy Class - mat and food toy used to full effect!"

Anna and Samson the Rhodesian Ridgeback puppy

And Ellen, who travels a lot with her work - and takes her Border Collie puppy with her - told me:

"The mat has helped greatly with making puppy trips easier and laying the foundations of good communication. Selkie's particularly great on her mat on buses, trains and in pubs!"

Finally, Wendy and Mike were delighted when their very active Vizsla pup learnt how to settle down on her mat:

"We've just come back from a couple of days on our narrowboat and Roux was so good! We went to a couple of pubs en route and used the mat and treats and she was as good as gold: she even went to sleep on it in a very noisy pub, ignoring yappy dogs and loud noises!"

I've given you a complete road map with detailed directions and GPS coordinates! Start from the beginning and follow the plan. Whenever something is not quite right, go back a step or two to where it was right, and move forward again.

In this Chapter we have established that:

- The mat can be used to get a number of calm responses - use your imagination!
- Your dog knows she's doing the right thing so there's no confusion
- Your dog can stay in any place you choose until you release her with "break!"
- It makes life much simpler and your dog's responses more consistent
- "I can wait patiently - I'm learning impulse control!"

Chapter 6
Surprise benefits of Mat Magic!

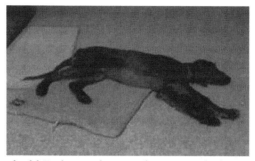

8-week-old Finley spark out on his mat in the living room

Your dog will now put herself on her mat, lie down, and wait. This is gradually going to turn into an action that sees your dog get on mat, lie down, R-E-L-A-X. You can teach your dog to totally relax at the flip of a switch.

Have you ever envied those people who, when finding they have to wait five or ten minutes for something, can just switch off and nap for a few minutes? They wake up refreshed and relaxed, ready to face whatever the world throws at them.

We were once travelling on a long car journey with a very successful businessman. He suddenly pulled over to a quiet spot at the side of the road and said, "I'm going to sleep for five minutes." He let his head loll and fell instantly asleep! Five minutes later, he opened his eyes, switched on the engine, and we continued our journey with a refreshed and renewed driver.

This is a skill your dog now has! And it's a skill I love to develop in my dogs.

Dogs need to sleep a massive number of hours a day. It's been established, by scientists studying stress in dogs, that the optimum number of hours of sleep for an adult dog is seventeen. Anything less and they start to get ragged. Puppies obviously need more sleep. Are you reeling from that revelation? If your dog is getting much less than seventeen hours you need to make some changes.

One of the huge advantages of the Magic Mat is that every time your dog gets on it she is relaxing and de-stressing. Even if she only goes on it for five minutes - like my businessman friend - she's getting the benefit of complete relaxation.

While I'm at my desk, my dogs are expected to find a bed or mat to concentrate on sleeping. Their sleep may be light or deep, but the state of relaxation induced by their mat ensures that they are truly resting. They are free of anxiety and totally content. When I'm out, I also expect them to be resting on their beds. I know they do because I've left my phone recording them. I get a rivettingly boring playback of a couple of hours of silence, interrupted by the occasional stretch, yawn, or creak of a bed.

Dogs can suffer a lot of stress in our human world. Granted, they get the great benefit of shelter, healthcare, and regular food, so it's a good trade-off for them - and it's why they hooked up with us in the first place. But the stress of our high-speed schedules can take a toll. If your dog is already struggling with anxiety or reacting poorly to new situations, people, or other dogs, then the seventeen hours of restorative sleep is even more important. So if your dog spends every minute of every day actively playing with the children, pacing about while you work, going for walks, jumping about in the living room, trying to steal food from the kitchen counters, nipping at heels, ripping toys up, digging, chasing, and barking, she is NOT leading the carefree, healthy, and happy life you may imagine.

Just like with a toddler, lack of rest demands its price. A toddler will grizzle, scream, become unreasonable, throw a tantrum, be demanding, impossible to satisfy, until you put her in her cot for a couple of hours' nap. Then she'll wake and be your angelic child once more. Dogs really are the same! Without the necessary sleep their poor stressed brains become overloaded. They become frantic, totally non-amenable to reason. They ignore what you are saying. They grab, nip, bark - they are beside themselves.

The answer is to escort them straight to their crate and settle them there quickly, then leave the room to allow them to sleep.

Ideally, you should build the sleep into their daily routine from the start!

How should our day go?

To give you an idea of how I manage my four - very, very different - dogs, this is an example of a day. There is no fixed schedule as my commitments vary throughout the week, but most of these things happen at some stage in the day.

- Rise, go out to garden, relieve themselves, and run about while I feed the hens
- Lie down in my bedroom or play with teddy bears while I dress
- Go outside again while I make coffee and feed the cat
- Each day a different dog comes for a solo roadwalk with me
- Lie down on their beds or quietly chew toys while I work
- Half an hour of very active games or training
- Rest while I have lunch
- Potter about with me while I do the washing, cleaning, and other chores
- Sleep while I go out to appointments - either in their crates in the van, or at home
- Highly active long dog walk with chasing, jumping, retrieving, and recall games
- Sleep till their supper time
- Potter, sleep, a few minutes training on and off, and so on

- Bedtime in their appointed sleeping places, where they stay till morning
- Training takes place a minute at a time at any time of day; garden visits every couple of hours; spontaneous active games any time

A carefully-considered sleep routine also means that my new puppies sleep through the night from the day they arrive at 7-8 weeks. That's something I'll go into more detail with you in another place. You can see from this, that building a strong association between the mat and sleep and rest, can aid your dog in speedily getting into that valuable relaxed state.

Your dog's behaviour around the house will improve dramatically. No nagging and poking, no cruising the tables and worktops for food, no doing naughty things to get a response from you. Your life together will become so much more harmonious and responsive.

All because of your Magic Mat.

In this Chapter we have established that:

- Your mat can induce a state of deep relaxation
- This relaxation will transfer to any bed
- Stress is massively lowered
- "Zzzzzz"

Conclusion

This is just the beginning for you!

If you've been working along as you read this book, you'll already have noticed a huge improvement in your dog's calmness and responsiveness. Congratulations! Now you see how well it works, you just have to keep it going, regularly.

Don't be tempted to chuck your mat aside and think, "I've done that. What next?" Keep it near to hand and remember that it can be the solution to a lot of common household problems and hysteria.

If you have a problem you need to resolve - if your dog has started doing something that annoys or frustrates you - revisit this book and see if your mat can help you to calm and slow things down enough to re-teach something you do like.

This is just the start for you!

There are just four skills you need to turn your wild puppy into your Brilliant Family Dog. Just four. Everything else flows from these. If you have these four skills, you're done!

You have in this book one quarter of what you need to have a Brilliant Family Dog. To find the other three parts, have a look at the Resources section at the end of this book.

Appreciation

I want to offer thanks to all those who have helped me get where I am with my dogs:

- First of all, my own long-suffering dogs! They have taught me so much when I've taken the time to listen.

- My students, who have shown me how they learn best, enabling me to give them what they need to know in a way that works for them.

- Some legendary teachers, principal amongst them: Sue Ailsby, Leslie McDevitt, Grisha Stewart, Susan Garrett. I wholeheartedly recommend them. They are trailblazers.

Resources

If you've enjoyed learning this key skill and you want to find the other three parts of the puzzle, go to www.brilliantfamilydog.com/books and pick up your next book!

Leave It! *How to teach Amazing Impulse Control to your Brilliant Family Dog - Book 2*

Let's Go! *Enjoy Companionable Walks with your Brilliant Family Dog - Book 3*

Here Boy! *Step-by-Step to a Stunning Recall from your Brilliant Family Dog - Book 4*

These cover the four skills you need to turn your wild puppy into your Brilliant Family Dog.

For a limited time, you can get the complete second book in this series absolutely free! Go to www.brilliantfamilydog.com/freebook and you will be reading it in just a few minutes.

And if you've got any specific queries, you can email me direct at beverley@brilliantfamilydog.com This will come straight to my personal inbox and I'll answer you - usually within 48 hours. Try me!

Meanwhile, for more free training, go to www.brilliantfamilydog.com and get a series of instructional emails on common day-to-day problems, like jumping up, chewing, barking, and so on.

Your emails are absolutely wonderful! I love them. Nobody else does anything like this. Maggie and Archie

I always enjoy reading your emails and find them really useful. Joss

The one thing Busta wasn't so good at was greeting people, but since your email we've had everyone popping in to try and put your tips into place and it worked! Now we no longer have him jumping all over us when we come through the door. Just a very happy dog sat down waggling his tail like mad, waiting for a fuss! Charlie and Busta

Love your Brilliant Family Dog course. I look forward to the nuggets! Jenny and Jazz

You talk such sense! I have been using the method you talk about so I can examine my almost 10 month old Beagle's teeth and it works a treat. You have inspired me to work towards clipping her dew claws myself instead of a visit to the vet! I'll let you know how I get on. I am sure there are many of us out there in the parent doggy world needing your expert tips. Alison and her Beagle pup

Your free book is waiting for you!

Get the next piece of the puzzle

Get the second book in this series absolutely free at

www.brilliantfamilydog.com/freebook

About the author

I've been training dogs for many years. First for competitive dog sports and over time to be stellar family pets. For most of my life, I've lived with up to four dogs, so I'm well used to getting a multi-dog household to run smoothly. It soon became clear that a force-free approach was by far the most successful, effective, and rewarding for me and the dogs. I've done the necessary studying for my various qualifications - for rehab of anxious and fearful "aggressive" dogs, early puppy development, and learning theory and its practical applications. I am continually studying and learning this endlessly amazing subject!

There are some superb teachers and advocates of force-free dog training, and you'll find those I am particularly indebted to in the Resources Section. Some of the methods I show you are well-known in the force-free dog training community, while many have my own particular twist.

A lot of my learning has come through the Puppy Classes, Puppy Walks, and Starter Classes I teach. These dog-owners are not looking for competition-standard training; they just want a Brilliant Family Dog they can take anywhere. Working with real dogs and their real owners keeps me humble - and resourceful! It's no good being brilliant at training dogs if you can't convey this enthusiasm and knowledge to the person the dog has to live with. So I'm grateful for everything my students have taught me about how they learn best.

Beverley Courtney BA(Hons) CBATI CAP2 MAPDT(UK) PPG

Printed in Great Britain
by Amazon